CYPRIAN KAMIL NORWID · SELECTED POEMS

CYPRIAN KAMIL
NORWID

Selected Poems

TRANSLATED BY
ADAM CZERNIAWSKI

with an introduction by
BOGDAN CZAYKOWSKI

ANVIL PRESS POETRY

Published in 2004
by Anvil Press Poetry Ltd
Neptune House 70 Royal Hill London SE10 8RF
www.anvilpresspoetry.com

ISBN 0 85646 369 8

This book is published
with financial assistance from
The Arts Council of England

A catalogue record for this book
is available from the British Library

Designed and set in Monotype Times New Roman by Anvil
Printed at Alden Press Limited
Oxford and Northampton

Contents

Late Poems
(1868–1881)

The Poet as 'Christian Socrates'

There lived in Paris ... a Polish writer little known in his own country, an artist known even less, a strange poet, a hiero-glyph-stylist, whose every poem has to be read syllable by syllable ten times over ... His ideas, despite his profound learning and detailed familiarity with the achievements of contemporary knowledge, move in a diametrically opposite direction to that of the modern philosophical current.

But he was not a dilettante, and certainly not a visionary, a mystic, or a lunatic ... He knew how to uncover in every thing such a relation of it to other things that it would become so original as to appear almost unrecognizable ...

He carried his soul around with him as if it were some kind of a numismatic rarity, unknown to anyone, unwanted, useless. Of less than middle height, lean, though shapely, with intelligent eyes ... he had in his manner the assurance and suavity of someone who had been in good society, and in his thoughts and words the roughness of ore burning with an inner fire. He resembled a stone salvaged from some marvel-lous edifice, which somewhere, sometime had burnt down completely.

JÓZEF TOKARZEWICZ (1884)

Truth embraces life and is therefore obscure, because it embraces a dark thing.

C. K. NORWID

Of the things of this world only two will remain,
Two only: *poetry and goodness* ... and nothing else ...

C. K. NORWID

THE COLD WAR made Eastern Europe an area of particular interest to West European nations, and the implosion of the Soviet empire has made it possible for a more extensive bridging of long-standing cultural as well as purely political divisions. A new configuration of a canonic character, drawn from disparate yet related traditions, all of which have at least indirect roots in Graeco-Roman and Judaeo-

Christian cultures, is gradually emerging. Much of this is being achieved by means of, to use Seamus Heaney's apt phrase, 'translated literature'.[1] Donald Davie, Michael Schmidt, and others, have pointed out some of the superficialities accompanying this process in regard to poetry: of 'talismanic presences' unsupported by real readership, or of contemporary translated verse floating on the fluctuations of political interest and ideological punditry in complete detachment from its traditions, as if it were preceded by a void. Yet readership of an inter-cultural character has been building up, and the voids are being gradually filled.

In the case of the Polish poetic tradition we have seen in the last few years the publication of four new translations of the masterpiece of 16th-century Polish Renaissance poetry, Jan Kochanowski's *Treny* (Laments), by Adam Czerniawski (revised version published by Legenda in Oxford), by Seamus Heaney and Stanisław Barańczak, by Barry Keane and by Michał Mikoś, and the appearance within the space of fifteen years of two volumes of translations of Cyprian Kamil Norwid (1821–1883), the most original of 19th-century Polish poets (the 1986 edition of Czerniawski's translations, published bilingually in Poland, and more recently Jerzy Peterkiewicz's, Christine Brooke-Rose's and Burns Singer's versions, published in 2000 by Carcanet in its Poetry Pleiade series).

Given the fact that both Peterkiewicz and Czerniawski are thoroughly naturalized British Poles, that both have translated Polish poetry and written extensively about it in English, a good way to begin a presentation of Norwid to readers unacquainted with his work, is to ask what were the reasons that made these two distinguished poets, critics and translators decide that Norwid's work should be added to the common treasury (as a 19th-century writer might have put it) of poetry in the English language.

Both translators had been attempting to break into the English readership with Norwid for a fairly long time.

---

1. Seamus Heaney, *The Government of the Tongue*, London 1988, p. 38.

Peterkiewicz's first translations of Norwid appeared as far back as 1958 in *Botteghe Oscure*, a sumptuous though little known magazine sponsored by an Italian aristocratic lady; Czerniawski's first translations appeared in a British school magazine as far back as the mid-1950s. Since those first publications both translators have kept on translating Norwid and publishing their translations intermittently in various periodicals and anthologies, and that despite the fact that Norwid's poetry is probably the most difficult a translator could face in any language.

In his introduction to the selection of Cyprian Norwid's *Poems – Letters – Drawings*, Peterkiewicz focuses first on the poet's life. He makes much of its vicissitudes and his rejection, as poet and artist (Norwid was also a painter and an interesting draughtsman) by the intellectual and literary Polish milieu of his time, a theme by now somewhat hackneyed in Norwid criticism, despite its basic validity. Indeed, Norwid's life was in many ways pitiful, and it ended in total neglect and oblivion in a Polish charitable institution near Paris. Perhaps the greatest pain of his life, apart from the increasing deafness to his poetry, and his acute realization of the extent to which material circumstances prevented him from fulfilling his intellectual and literary potential, was the fact that he did not find a woman ready to share his life (and he considered women to be the measure of a society's worth). His literary career, however, had begun with great promise in Warsaw around 1840, and continued in this way for a few years after he had to leave Warsaw for the West in 1842, having been associated with a circle of young conspirators who plotted against Russian rule over Poland. Those early years, when Norwid was considered by a small group of Polish aristocrats and literati almost a man of genius, ended in rejection and bitterness. In 1852 Norwid travelled via London to America in search of employment, only to return, again via London, to Paris in 1854. There, he tried for the rest of his life to convince readers that he had something important to say, and that his poems charted a new direction in Polish poetry, as he claimed in a preface to his *Vade-mecum* (a title typical for Norwid), a collection of a hundred lyrics. But the volume was not published until 1953 and, to augment the irony, not in Poland but in Tunbridge Wells! It was not until the early 1900s that Norwid's poetry was rediscovered and pronounced at least equal to that of Adam Mickiewicz and Juliusz Słowacki, the two other major 19th-century Polish poets. That rediscovery set a seal on much of subsequent Norwid criticism, as it made him into a symbol of the artist as victim of philistine society. Peterkiewicz makes much of Norwid as the rejected artist, without really grasping the true nature of Norwid's fate and character. But it is clear that one of the reasons for his sustained attempt to make Norwid known in English is the desire to be an instrument of what Norwid himself had hoped for: the correcting hand of time.

Peterkiewicz's other justification has more to do with Norwid's poetry. He describes him as a great innovator in Polish poetry and a profoundly original sensibility. He grants that there is 'some inherent obscurity' in Norwid's work, but suggests that it 'results not so much from the allusive and metaphoric congestions of his style but rather from the didactic emphasis which, aiming inward, almost ceases to be didactic.' What he finds especially innovative and valuable in Norwid's poetry is the fact that Norwid reversed 'the usual didactic practices by imposing a poetic sequence on a moral and not vice versa ... [T]he imposition is such that the reader has no alternative but to accept the hidden message, whereas one merely acknowledges with a nod a moral tag attached to an eighteenth-century fable, satire or verse-letter.'[2] Though Peterkiewicz comes close to the mark here, he does not explain how Norwid achieves 'the reverse' of traditional didactic verse. And his insistence on treating Norwid as primarily a didactic poet misrepresents in a significant way Norwid's 'Socratic' temper, his desire 'to uncover in every thing such a relation of it to other things

---

2. Cyprian Norwid, *Poems – Letters – Drawings*, ed. and trans. Jerzy Peterkiewicz, Manchester 2000, p. xiv.

that it would become so original as to appear almost unrecognizable.' Norwid was a questioning, non-conformist, 'sincere' poet (in Verlaine's sense of the term), and he tried to emulate not only Socratic virtues, such as his civic courage and integrity, but also what he took to be his method of dialogic subversion of received or unexamined opinion. At the same time Norwid's questioning was, as it happened, rooted firmly in the teachings of Christ, something which Peterkiewicz avoids mentioning altogether.

Very much aware of the need to go beyond a mere assertion of Norwid's stature, Czerniawski brings a new perspective to the evaluation of Norwid's work. In his 'Afterword' to his translations of Norwid's poetry he asks a most pertinent question, while taking for granted the assumption it is based on: 'How can a translator verify Norwid's genius? Norwid is a nineteenth-century poet as well as a precursory author. How then can one introduce the work of a poet, who is simultaneously grounded in nineteenth-century traditions, and who at the same time shatters them? ... How to convey then to the English-language reader of the late twentieth century, that the poet he is reading is not only expressing the consciousness of the second half of the nineteenth century, but also proclaiming the poetry of the twentieth century.' And he answers himself: 'One should reveal Norwid's *originality.*' Norwid – he adds – 'cannot appear as a second-rate Hopkins, Browning, Clough; or as an imitation of Emily Dickinson ... '.[3]

The names Czerniawski lists were chosen not without reason; there are indeed some parallels between Norwid and these writers. But these parallels do not get us very far. Norwid is a very different poet from Hopkins (which Czerniawski points out himself), so that the only significant similarities (apart from both of them being viewed as premoderns) are their religious orthodoxy and the successful way in which they managed not to let their poetry succumb

---

3. Cyprian Kamil Norwid, *Poezje/Poems*, trans. Adam Czerniawski, Kraków 1986, p. 129.

to the dangers inherent in that fact. As for Browning, the similarity can only be between the two poets' longer poems, and this is slight. There are perhaps certain parallels in some of Norwid's poems with Clough's heavy-duty lines, but there is nothing in Clough that would make anyone want to compare him with Emily Dickinson, whereas Norwid has been compared to her by more than one critic, and this time with some justification. Norwid is as laconic and elliptical as Dickinson, and there are now and again uncanny analogies in the effect he achieves by condensation. A further similarity is Norwid's mastery, in many of his poems, of traditional form, which is not only Dickinsonian but almost Poundian in the energy with which rhythm, metre and syntax both carry and contain compressions of thought (perhaps the closest parallel is 'Hugh Selwyn Mauberley', and perhaps one of the influences in both Norwid's and Pound's instances is Théophile Gautier). In an excellent Norwid poem, as in the case of an excellent Dickinson poem, distillation of thought and distillation of form seem to coalesce, become one.

Czerniawski uses the example of Norwid's 'Why Not in Chorus?' to point to the striking similarities between a Dickinson and a Norwid poem. In his introduction to the anthology *The Burning Forest* he quotes Emily Dickinson's

> Not one of all the purple Host
> Who took the Flag today
> Can tell the definition
> So clear of Victory
>
> As he defeated – dying –
> On whose forbidden ear
> The distant strains of triumph
> Burst agonized and clear!

In reading this poem, he says, 'one has the uncanny feeling that one is reading English-language equivalents of Norwid's poems,' for this poem 'is equivalent in tone, style and imagery to Norwid's "Out of Harmony"'.[4] Indeed, it is:

1

Round *God's* manger
The chosen sing;
But others at the door
Silently catch their breath . . .

2

And what of those
Just entering the town
Where the ear still rings
With *innocents' cries!* . . .

3

Sing you! who are chosen
There where He was born;
My ear is pierced
By the pursuing horn . . .

4

Sing in triumphant chorus
Your praises unto God – –
I? – could spoil your song:
I have seen *blood!* . . . [5]

Granted the similarities, there are also significant differences between the two poets. Norwid is a poet whose thought is largely historicist and shaped by an acute awareness of civilizational and social factors. His notion and use of irony make of it more than a figure of speech; it is, for him, being's inseparable shadow, a mode or condition of all human endeavour. His use of genre and form in the shorter poems is richer, and reflects a familiarity with the gnomic, classical, Renaissance and baroque traditions.

---

4. Adam Czerniawski, ed. and trans., *The Burning Forest: Modern Polish Poetry*, Newcastle-upon-Tyne, 1988. The title 'Out of Harmony' has in this edition been changed to 'Why Not in Chorus?'.
5. This and all subsequent translations are by Adam Czerniawski.

Another difference is that Dickinson did not write long poems, nor did she write plays, which Norwid did, displaying his originality there, too. Their innovative character can perhaps be best conveyed by saying that, while owing something to Shakespeare, they resemble the drawing-room plays of T. S. Eliot (while being poetically more exciting than Eliot's), the symbolist plays of Yeats, but with perhaps a stronger intellectual theme, as well as some modernist drama, in which little seems to happen, and yet a sort of revolution in consciousness and sensibility is achieved.

He also wrote short stories and prose pieces, which he called 'Black flowers', that constitute a separate minor genre (Norwid's use of genres is, in fact, quite unusual), of which a particularly fine example is his piece on Chopin. Moreover, as far as poetry is concerned, Norwid did not confine himself to short lyrics, but wrote a number of longer poems, some of which are in a lyrical vein (of which an excellent example is his 'Chopin's Piano') while others are discursive, narrative and essayistic. Among the latter perhaps the most interesting and accomplished is 'Quidam' (a quasi-narrative poem whose setting is Rome 'on the eve of Christian revelation'), but several others, although uneven or fragmentary, contain brilliant insights, striking formulations of complex ideas, and passages of great poetic beauty.

His range is thus much broader than that of Dickinson. A further, and very important dissimilarity, is Norwid's use of colloquial language, which puts him closer to Laforgue, one of Eliot's models, and to Eliot himself. One of the effects of this feature is the achievement in Norwid's verse of what might be termed 'formal dissonance', aided by Norwid's peculiar use of punctuation, which at times, instead of helping to order the sequencing of meaning, disrupts the flow of verse so that the written, structured language is transformed into articulated speech, as if the author were delivering his poems to an audience, and dramatizing/gesturing for emphasis or irony.

A further interesting aspect of infusing the conventional, formal scripted work with the oral is Norwid's use of pauses, which reflected his view of silence as a part of speech and of meaning (when the reader or listener becomes more of a participant in discourse by no longer listening, or reading, but being delivered, as it were, to his own thought). Norwid was thus highly conscious that by rejecting mellifluousness, melodiousness, unity of tone, the poeticisms and bardic high style, he was subverting the models of Polish lyrical verse. 'Perfect lyric poetry' – he wrote – 'should be like a plaster cast: those rough edges where forms cross each other and leave cracks should be left intact and not smoothed over . . . '

Although Norwid was a great admirer of Chopin's music, championing him, for instance, in his poetic treatise 'Promethidion' as a supreme example of a great artist, who 'lifted the folkloric [national] to the universal' through his art, he nevertheless often thought of poetry in sculptural (even lapidary) rather than musical terms. That the two forms of art have a profound element in common (which, if you think of it, is not at all counter-intuitive), is perhaps an idea that informs Norwid's lyric 'Lapidaria':

Sculpture's
Whole secret:
A spirit – like lightning
In gesture caught – –

Marvels and wonders
And lifts its tiny palms
From this world's cradle
Towards the still uncaptured
In infinite space!

Only she who nurses
And he who's held a chisel;
Only she who dances
And he who's held an arm:
They only – and the earth's
Bosom sensing rain
Move the spirit's veil
– – Into a thrilling swirl!

II

The Truth must dazzle gradually
Or every man be blind –

EMILY DICKINSON

THE PROBLEM OF Norwid's obscurity has been a persistent one, and cannot be simply wished away. It must be tackled head on, if we are to take true measure of his achievement. Norwid was more than aware of what was being said and written about him, both in print and in private correspondence among his 'friends'. At one point he responded to it in 'Obscurity':

I

He complains my speech is dark –
Has he ever lit the taper?
That remained his servant's task
(The many reasons hid from us).

2

The spark ignites the wick,
The melting wax engulfs the flame,
Its star-light slowly drowns,
Its sheen now bluish, on the wane.

3

You quickly think it lost
In the consummating flow –
Grant it faith, not just sparks and ash:
With your faith . . . see how it glows!

4

You, who grudge a wretched moment –
Know the nature of my songs:
Their sacrificial flame will blaze
When the epoch's chill is gone!

If we do what the poem tells us to do, it yields a clear meaning. It asks for a reading that runs counter to reading 'in haste/under the rule of Print-Pantheism'. And it asks for trust. It promises a reward for trustful, attentive and participatory reading. That reward in Norwid (and he knew about it) is more than just a meaning. That reward is a thought that makes a difference to how we view ourselves and the world. And which at the same time recognizes how difficult it is to be meaningful.

There are in Norwid numerous observations of a hermeneutical, semantic, almost semiotic character. He thought of himself as a reader of signs, of traces left by God for human beings to recognize and decipher. His longer poems and dramas both grope for a meaning that is elusive, yet important, and create a movement towards it, a sort of argument that the reader participates in throughout. This is particularly striking in a group of shorter poems in which a recasting of meaning occurs when you have read the last line. This recasting results in a re-interpretation of the meaning of earlier lines, so that the end of the poem induces a retrospective movement of thought. A good example is 'The Sphinx':

> The Sphinx barred my way in a dark cave
> Ever hungry for truths
> Like a taxman, beggar or knave
> Molesting travellers with cries of 'Truth!'
>
> *
>
> 'Man? . . . he's an ignorant callow
> Priest . . . '
> I replied
>
> *
>
> And marvelling saw
> The Sphinx pressed against the rock:
> I slipped past alive!

The action which the poem describes results in a new, and ironic, interpretation of man's reply to the Sphinx, who accepts the statement as true. And this in turn reflects on the first stanza and re-evaluates the concept of the Sphinx. Indeed, the mystery of the world demands answers of man, but his answers are far from satisfactory.

A closer look at 'The Sphinx' reveals still another characteristic feature which is crucial in understanding Norwid's poetry. Clearly, the poem is a parable. In fact, the parabolic character of Norwid's writings, including his shorter poems, is one of its most important generic and formal aspects. And it is the nature of parabolic writing or speech that it requires the listener or reader to participate in the construing of its meaning and furthermore, that it aims at questioning and subverting views and opinions that have broad currency and acceptance, and in effect seeks to change them.

Norwid's poetry, whatever the analogies with other poets, is *sui generis*. And so was Norwid himself, a wholly idiosyncratic person, who cultivated idiosyncrasy not because he wanted to, but because it was thrust upon him by his marginalization and his highly individual perspective. And it was precisely this perspective, questioning and reverent at the same time, that lay at the bottom of his ironic mode, in fact, of his poetics. It is paradoxical that a poet who was a thorough Catholic believer, that is, a believer in a universalizing and still in his time widely embraced set of convictions and teachings, found in it such an intellectual place for himself that it caused him to be cast outside orthodoxy; not the orthodoxy of Catholicism's fundamental outlook but the orthodoxy of its shallow and obfuscated misapplication and opinion. The paradox is explained by Norwid's conscious imitation of Christ.

Read what your Saviour said to the Pharisees ... and you will see that you will not find a more colossal irony anywhere, either in the past or now. Even the form, questioning rather than asserting, is purely ironic! Yes, my dear, I am not ashamed of irony, for it is enough for a servant to be like his Master, and for the disciple to be like his Teacher. I won't correct the Saviour, that I won't.[6]

Norwid's Socratic Christliness enabled him to put in its proper place: evil, death, sickness, irony, beauty, prayer, and originality, which last he defined as 'being incrementally faithful to one's sources'.

Faithful he definitely was, both in his view of humanity and of the historical moment in Western civilization into which he was born and which he viewed from the vantage point of an apparently superfluous man (the 'supernumerary actor', as he called himself), and in terms of his poetics.

BOGDAN CZAYKOWSKI

6. Cyprian Norwid, *Pisma wszystkie* [Collected Works], ed. Juliusz Gomulicki, Warsaw 1971, Vol. 8 p. 186.

SOME COMMENTARIES

Adam Czerniawski (ed.), *The Mature Laurel*, Bridgend 1991

George Gömöri, *Cyprian Norwid*, New York 1974

George Gömöri and Bolesław Mazur (eds), *Norwid: Poet – Thinker – Craftsman*, London 1988

Hans Robert Jauss, 'Norwid and Baudelaire as Contemporaries' in P. Sterer (ed.), *The Structure of the Literary Process*, Amsterdam 1982

Manfred Kridl, *A Survey of Polish Literature and Culture*, The Hague 1956

Czesław Miłosz, *The History of Polish Literature*, London 1969

Jerzy Peterkiewicz, 'Introducing Norwid', *Slavonic and East European Review*, November 1948

Reference Guide to World Literature, Vol. 1, 3rd edn, New York and London 2003

Translator's Note

I HAVE SCRUPULOUSLY followed Norwid's idiosyncratic punctuation and quirky use of italics. Wherever possible, I attempted to reproduce, at least partially, his rhyming patterns. But I have avoided rhymes wherever this practice would result in padding or distortions of meaning. I have written at length about the problems of translating Norwid in my preface to *The Burning Forest* and in 'Translation of Poetry: Theory and Practice' (*Modern Poetry in Translation*, No. 15 (1999). I have annotated a few of the poems with essential information.

The middle section of this volume consists of a selection from the *Vade-mecum* sequence. The manuscript originally had a hundred poems. It was never published in the poet's lifetime, and when it was eventually recovered, some pages were missing, some mutilated, some emended, not always very legibly. Juliusz Gomulicki, Norwid's distinguished and indefatigable editor, has provided readings of the emendations and has conjecturally filled in the gaps with a handful of unassigned poems. I have here followed Gomulicki's decisions, but they had to be accepted on faith, because there can now be no conclusive evidence to support them.

One of the *Vade-mecum* poems is the substantial 'Chopin's Piano', which I felt unable to translate. So, knowing Norwid's great admiration for the composer, I have instead translated the piece on Chopin from *Black Flowers*, the poet's collection of sketches of his celebrated contemporaries, whom he had visited just before their deaths, that also includes Adam Mickiewicz and Juliusz Słowacki. It has the quality of a prose-poem.

I have been working on Norwid translations since my schooldays. As a result of decades of experience, of sustained critical comments by Ann Czerniawska, and latterly by Agata Brajerska-Mazur, many of these translations have over the years been undergoing varying degrees of revision.

But my greatest debt is to Bogdan Czaykowski, to his poetic sensibility and his deep understanding of Norwid, which he generously shared with me. More recently, some of these translations have also been severely tested in seminars at the Universities of Gdańsk, Kraków and Toruń. Consequently, many of the versions published here differ, at times quite drastically, from those published earlier. The satisfaction of working on the final stages of this life-long project was greatly enhanced by the generous hospitality of Anna Lubicz-Łuba and Gilbert Bartholomew at Lions Bay in Canada; of Drue Heinz at Casa Ecco on Lake Como; and by a Ledig-Rowohlt fellowship at Château Lavigny in Switzerland.

A number of these translations have appeared, often in earlier versions, in *Poezje/Poems*, my bilingual selection of Norwid's poetry published in Poland; in my anthology *The Burning Forest*, in *The Rialto*, *Modern Poetry in Translation*, *The Poetry Review*, *The SHOp* and *Metre*.

A. CZ.

Monmouth, Wales, June 2003

Early Poems
(1847–1861)

Reality

It was evening: they were reading
Shakespeare's play called *Death of Julius Caesar*,
And though the gathering knew that masterpiece,
Yet would either fall silent together,
Trembling, or wouldn't all listen together,
And were like a harp in the Master's hands.
The air was balmy towards dusk, windows
Open to the balcony drew laurel scent indoors,
And from above – a hazy crown of white stars
In that constellation which, having fallen
To the side of the Milky Way, is called Sobieski's
Shield.

     They read the well-known scene:
The night-scene in lonely Brutus's tent
When he set his sword to pen sarcasm
About virtue. So when I say, 'They were like a harp',
I am borrowing from Shakespeare, who's calling the boy
To play to Brutus in this very scene,
And then to make him sleep and bring forth a vision.
The vision came, since memory no longer feels,
Having first disappeared, string by string, beneath the
     fingers
Of the boy falling asleep. This is the youth,
Apparently a page, that Shakespeare used as a tool
For experience – then fell silent and ghosts enter,
Even though the writer had no trick in mind.
– Simply was creative – the logic of creation is not ours –
That's why so wondrously mysterious that many
Think it naught. He composed – just as a goblet
Full to the brim repeats the high heavenly blue
And sheds its liquid only when tears
Should fall upon liquid-reflected clouds,
Tears not used to measure but rather to brim over.

Archimedes had not sought the crowning calculation
When he entered the public baths,
For creation is both certainty and chance,
Accidental to the outside, internally coherent.
When conscience sees it, it will appear to you
Made up of settled merits, until fulfilled,
Being like a just crown of labour;
From the outside Creativity will indeed strike you
As a gift of heavenly generosity and a crooked line
Without which the straight seems lifeless;
A line representing revolt in geometry,
But it ensures that geometry is exploited,
Otherwise it would be an illiterate sign,
Undoubtedly a certain kind of puzzle!

So they read it as an imaginative work, but being familiar,
They would interrupt it and restart the reading –
Until after Caesar came the Republic
And the politics of the period, which one touches
With that thunder of words still painful and obscure,
Which history by-passes and reality muddles.
With judgment of the serious, with hearts of forgotten
    men,
Uniting them annually over what they had quarrelled.
'Oh, experience – Robert was saying – experience,
What are you to us? Let's look closely,
For, not being too old, we can push back remembrance
Beyond us: a hundred battlefields, four rebellions,
And all our youth spent in reading
Despatches about various insurrections.
And amongst themselves the blue-blooded, like
    cornflowers,
Say: *From the last to the very latest incidents* –
And before you've uttered that Christian date,
It's already changed! – times rich in *incidents*.
 – Would they were in thoughts, virtues and accomplished
    aims!

– Oh, do not watch babies sleeping in their cots,
Do not reflect on youngsters' games,
Don't be a father, don't count yourself amongst sons,
Don't, being a nanny, amuse a babe,
For you die selfish, leaving – pains!
And nought besides. –'

      He spoke and with his hand sought the heart,
Calm like a surgeon, like a murderer pale,
For he knew they would reply, 'Be a god!',
And he felt at once those truths were a monologue.
Hearing these words, Theodore spoke in a different vein:
'Humanity calls for sacrifice – humanity's collective,
When an individual is ill or dying,
She walks on – a strong and healthy wench.
Occasionally, one or other will push away doctors,
Leap over the grave,
And move on – this is reality's law:
Be a god! or don't come here with a face pale
Like a sickle catacomb moon – Humanity's grown up.'
'I admit – Robert replied – she is a tough lady,
But, I can't conclude she's sensitive and lofty
Nor would I call progress what retreats into paganism –
I even forbid Reality to call Energy
Which only knows it's in a chase!'

'How then?' – 'What is it?' – they all cried:
'Thus quickly you've concluded
To differ about reality itself?
If so – that's the end. We could have continued,
But if you differ even in this regard,
That what one calls life, another styles death,
That's too much – let's rather read Shakespeare.'

'Let's!' – then silence –

Someone's opening
The window which Robert left ajar – someone
Wrapped in a cloak –

            'Ha! ha! he's come to haunt us' –
'Guess who it is!' – they call and urge
The silent figure not to pull back
The velvet hood – –

            'Be assured, gentlemen –
The guest replies – no one will guess! I say it myself,
I'm mindful to keep my head covered,
And I won't bore you long – I go – will not tarry –'
Uttering these words slowly, he sat at table,
Propped his head on his hand, while the hood
Folded over his brow, cast a shadow on his face;
And his elbow pressed against
That opened Shakespeare tome.

They were silent, half-smiling, 'I represent
Doubt about Reality – said the uninvited guest –
For, if, for instance, the fatherly shade
Were to appear to the Prince and say, as in Shakespeare,
"This whole court and train are but a dream,
And all that sheen that licks the armour
Like a snake – and these banners, and that
Whole reality, all that is but a dream"[1] –
And, if, I say, he were to describe each thing truly
As it is – first maidens would call him mad,
Then the flatterers, then the courtiers,
Then the empty skulls – then – graveyard
Birds – and people would throw bones at him,
Crying: "Ideologue! He's spoiling reality,
For he's mad" – such a graveyard tragedy

Would be played, played at little expense –
Cheaper today than this Shakespeare tome – –'

                                    – – Here
He chuckled, then stretched his hand towards the balcony,
Plucked a flower and bent over the calyx
Like one who favours a clean scent, or dreams and sighs.

At this Theodore called: 'The lamp's flickering, gentlemen!
Lights!' – and at once the candelabrum,
Resting on a Sphinx's bronzed head, vanished – they rang:
And after an interval as silent as brief
A servant ran in with another twin-like candelabrum
Bearing a Sphinx's head – a gilded head.

Written in 1847

My Song

POLONIUS: *I'll speak to him again*
What do you read, my lord? . . .
HAMLET: *Words, words, words!*

— SHAKESPEARE

That black thread spins
Behind, in front and near,
In every sigh,
In every smile,
In tears, prayers and hymns . . .

*

Too strong to sever,
Errant or sacred,
I'd rather not break it;
Yet always wherever
It's with me for ever:
In a book that's open,
Or binding the flowers;
Or sliding, shimmering
Like webs in Autumn
That gradually fray,
Then grow again
A link in the chain.

*

I'll win in the end
Not sob like a child:
Hand me the cup and wreath! . . .
I put on that crown
And I drained the lees:
They called me a clown!

*

I raised my arm
To seek my heart,
The hand grew cold:
They laughed aloud,
I lost a hand
In a black band.

*

That black thread spins
Behind, in front and near,
In every sigh,
In every smile,
In tears, prayers and hymns . . .

*

I'll win in the end
Not sob like a child;
My golden lute,
May it help me yet
Summon the songs
Of the Czarnolas bard[2]
To restore my heart!
So I plucked the strings . . .
                    . . . but worse grew the hurt.

Written in Florence, 1844

Beauty

... God sees all –

          'How can
God's eye endure ugliness all round?'
– If you wish to know, with an artist's eye
Look closely at a ruin, at cobwebs
In sunlight, at matted straw
In fields, at potter's clay – –
– He gave us all, even His traces,
As He perceives things, shows no envy, needs no shame!
Yet there is sun-gilded Pride
Convinced the sun will not pierce her;
She is the end of sight and contemplation,
She is the screen against God's rays,
So that man, the most ungrateful creature in the world,
Should feel extinguished brightness and night in his
     eyes.
– In every art let all arts gleam, save the one
Through which the work is to be done.

In an Album

(In Warsaw)

– If instead of windows so amply
Frozen to precious stones we had
A few statues against azure skies,
Or a niche in a columned peristyle for reveries . . .
If only *Sorrento* sunlight
Would slither through laurel leaves:
Ah well! . . . here all is veiled in mists . . .

(In Rome)

– If instead of this lovely cypress
And glare that hurts the eyes
And the Colosseum (red foxes' lair!)
One could glimpse the plaits of a weeping willow,
And instead of a land of rubble and ashes
And shattered Etruscan pots, see irrigated
Fields of water-melon
And just touch a little Polish soil . . .
Ah well! . . .

      Oh imagination! . . . Lady Penelope,
I know you – as when your nimble foot
Skips over your suitors' ashen hearts . . .
I know you – and your mottled fan,
Your gesture – the sweet descants' chant,
Your power – and *truth* – and – I rest content . . .

Their Strength

Epigram

Valiant commanders, armies fully trained,
Police – male, female, uniformed and plain –
Thus united against whom? –
A few thoughts . . . that aren't new! . . .

A Funeral Rhapsody in Memory of General Bem[3]

Iusiurandum patri datum usque at hanc diem
ita servavi . . .

— HANNIBAL

I

Why ride away, Shadow, hands broken on the mail,
Torch sparks playing about your knees? –
Green with laurels, the sword spattered with candle tears,
The falcon strains, your horse stamps its foot like a dancer.
– Banners in the wind blow and lash against each other
Like moving tents of nomad armies in the sky.
Long trumpets shudder in sobbing and pennants
Bow their wings which droop from above
Like spear-pierced dragons, lizards and birds . . .
Like the many ideas you sought with your spear . . .

II

Mourning maidens go, some raising their arms
Filled with fragrant sheaves sundered by the wind;
Some gather into shells tears breaking from the cheek,
Some still seek the road *built centuries ago* . . .
Others dash against the earth huge pots of clay
Whose clatter in cracking yet deepens the sorrow.

III

Boys strike hatchets azured by the sky,
Serving lads strike light-burnished shields,
A mighty standard sways through the smoke, its
    spear-point
Seemingly leaning against the vaulted heavens . . .

IV

They plunge into a canyon . . . and emerge in moonlight
Black against the sky, an icy glare brushed them,
Glimmering on blades of spears like a star unable to fall,
The chant suddenly ceased, then splashed out like
    a wave . . .

V

On – on – till it's time to slide into the grave
And we'll behold a black chasm that lurks ahead,
Which mortals can never transgress,
A spear will prod your steed – like an old spur . . .

VI

And we shall draw the cortège, saddening slumber-seized
    cities,
Battering gates with urns, whistling on blunted hatchets,
Till the walls of Jericho tumble down like logs,
Swooned hearts revive – nations clear the must from their
    eyes . . .

. . . .

On – on – –

1851

On Board the *Margaret Evans*
Sailing This Day to New York

London 1852, December, 10 am

I

Occasional sun-squibs glisten on sails,
Brush the masts and splash on waves;
Mists disappear like *a woman's veil*,
Behind it rise *ruin-like* clouds! . . .

II

'Why ruins? and why a veil?
Why a woman's? . . . ' – let the critic demand,
Let him blame the Muse for the muddied
Concept-harmony of her mind –

III

I – don't know . . . I see and sketch this sadly
As though I were one of the flying cranes
That drag their shadow across the sails
Not thinking *whether any trace remains!* . . .

IV

I don't know . . . the end, I perhaps never do,
But . . .
    (here the helmsman cried)
        . . . Adieu! . . .

[Such depths]

In the Ocean such depths there are
That waves surging from below
Reject the lead-tipped rope,
　　For here ends the plumb-line's rule ...
Now at the mercy of the sun and stars,
You don't ask land how the run will end ...

1857

To Emir Abd el Kader in Damascus[4]

Praise of living virtuous men
Is like praising God himself,
And good news received with love
Is like the Ghost in Mary's womb.

Accept then, Sir, a distant tribute,
You, who are like a shield of God;
May an orphan's tears, a cripple's tears
Shine as baptism on your head.

The one God reigns from age to age,
None knows the measure of His favours;
He bids the nails drop from his wounds,
He orders stars to shine as spurs;

His foot is in the rainbow's stirrup,
He rides to Judgment day;
Who gave Him earth and sky?
Who gave Him light and shade?

And if in tears of tortured men,
If in innocent maidens' blood,
If in the waking child,
There is only the one God,

Then let your tent be broader
Than David's cedar groves;
For of the Magi you were first
To mount your horse upon the hour!

Yesterday-and-I

A deafness sad and rare –
When you hear
The Word – but miss
The accent and *stress* . . .

*

For an angel calls . . . But they mock:
'*Thunder!*'
So you slam the coffin lid over your face under
The rock.

*

You have no wish to cry
'Eloi . . . Eloi . . . ' – why?
– Ah, God! . . . sails lap up the northern gale.
Seas rail.

*

A hum in my ear (I have no theory
Regarding storms)
So I dream and feel a folio of history
Turn to stone . . .

26 [27] December 1860

My Country

Those who say my country means:
Meadows, flowers and fields of wheat,
Hamlets and trenches – must confess
    These – are her feet.

The child – not snatched from his mother's arms;
The youth – at her side will grow;
And she leans on her adult son:
    These – are my laws.

My country has not risen *here*;
My body antedates the Flood,
My spirit soars over Chaos:
    I pay rent to the world.

No nation fashioned or saved me;
I recall eternity's span;
David's key unlocked my lips,
    Rome called me man.

I fall on the sand to wipe with my hair
My country's blood-stained feet:
But I know her face and crown
    Radiant like the sun of suns.

My ancestors have known no other;
Her feet with my hand I used to feel;
I often kissed the peasant sandal strap
    Round her heel.

They needn't teach me where my country lies;
Hamlets, trenches and fields of wheat,
Flesh and blood and this her scar
    Are her print, her feet.

Paris, January 1861

Marionettes

I

Wouldn't you be bored when a million
Silent stars shine around the world,
Each sparkling in a different mould,
All still – yet flying? . . .

2

Still the earth – the aeons vast,
And those living at this hour
Of whom not a bone will last,
Though men will be as now . . .

3

Wouldn't you be bored on a stage
So amateurish and small,
Where everyone's Ideals rage
And the show is paid with life? –

4

Truly, how is one to kill the time,
I am most sincerely bored;
What remedy, Madam, should I explore,
Shall I write prose or rhyme? –

5

Or write nothing . . . just sit in the sun
Absorbed in that fine romance:
Composed by the Flood upon grains of sand,
Doubtless for the amusement of man(!) –

6

Or better still – I know a braver way
Against this damned *ennui*:
Forget *people*, call on *persons*, wear
A neatly fastened tie! . . .

1861

Memento

I

In a mediaeval castle once I saw
Oak doors hung on elegant hinges
Shaped like an eagle hammered out of nails:
So when the wind rushing through the terrace
Swung the massive portals,
The eagle torn in half swayed to and fro,
Moaning hoarsely with the rust of years,
Longing to wrench its nail-gripped wings.

II

The ruins' guardian and night passers-by
Confused the screeching hinges
With souls' lamentations over unknown crimes;
Poets described them with pen and ink;
Tourists, having closely spied the door,
Would – if the hinge stayed mute –
Carve a remarkable date or celebrated name:
Here – '*Lola Montez*' – there – '*The Margrave
Boissy*', sometimes *Two Hearts*, '*Speranza!*'
'*Nadar*', '*Washington Irving*', '*Sancho Panza*',
'*Jack the Wanderer from Pinsk*', and so on . . .
Signing with their knives.

III

But when above the tower golden flashes
Spark, accompanying heavy thunderous clouds,
No one dares touch the portals – as if it were
The Zion rock – standing aside, terrified,
Hearing the creaking of the growling portals,
The crunch of eagles – like an armoured troop
    in flight! . . .

IV

'Thus – between the breath of Asia and the West . . .'
Said I . . . and thought to carve a rhyme
In oak . . . and artfully score my name and crest
Containing *an anchor* or *two doves*
So that a great historian . . . might recall
That when I came here . . . I owned a blade.

[Give me a blue ribbon . . .]

Give me a blue ribbon – I will hand it back
Without delay . . .
Or give me the shadow of your supple neck:
– No! not the shadow.

The shadow will change when you wave,
It does not lie.
Now there is nothing I desire, lovely maid,
I take my arm away . . .

God's past rewards
Were lesser things:
A leaf stuck to a window pane,
A drop of rain.

from
Black Flowers
(1856)

Chopin

And – later – later – in Paris Frederick Chopin was living in rue Chaillot which, when you walk up from the Champs Elysées, in the left-hand row of houses, on the first floor, has apartments with windows facing gardens, the Pantheon cupola, and the whole of Paris ... the only point with a collection of views somewhat approaching those you find in Rome. And such was the apartment that Chopin had with such a view, whose main part consisted of a huge drawing-room with two windows, where his immortal piano stood, a piano you wouldn't describe as exquisite – resembling a wardrobe or a chest of drawers, excellently decorated like the fashionable pianos – but rather quite triangular, long, three-legged, which now, I believe, is hardly ever found in elegant apartments. In this drawing-room Chopin used to have his meals at five, and would then descend, as best he could, down the stairs, and drive to the Bois de Boulogne, from whence, when he returned, they would carry him upstairs, since he could not walk up on his own.

Many times I had meals with him thus and accompanied him on drives. On one such occasion we made a flying visit to Passy where Bohdan Zaleski lived. We didn't go upstairs as there was no one to carry Chopin, but stayed in the little garden in front of the house where the then quite small son of the poet played on the lawn ...

A long time passed since that event, and I stopped calling on Chopin, although keeping myself informed always how he was, and knowing that his sister had arrived from Poland. Until one day I did call with the intention of seeing him, but a French maid said he was asleep; I left a visiting card and slipped out quietly.

Hardly had I descended a few steps when the maid appears behind me saying that Chopin, when he learnt who had called, was inviting me in – that, in other words, he wasn't asleep but had merely no wish to receive visitors. So I entered the room adjoining the drawing-room, where Chopin had his bedroom, feeling very grateful that he wished to see me, and found him dressed but half-reclining on the bed, his legs swollen, which I could discern at once because of the shoes and stocking he was wearing. The artist's sister sat at his side, strangely like him in profile . . . He, in the shadow of deep bed with curtains, propped up on pillows, and wrapped in a shawl, looked very beautiful, as always, displaying in the most mundane movements something of perfection, something of a monumental outline . . . something which either Athenian aristocracy could have adopted as a cult during the most beautiful epoch of Greek civilization – or that which an artist of dramatic genius portrays, for instance, in classical French tragedies, which because of their theoretical polish, in no way resemble the world of antiquity, but can nevertheless, thanks to the genius of a Rachel, become naturalized, credible and truly classical . . . Chopin possessed such naturally idealized perfection of gestures, wherever and how ever I saw him . . .

So – his voice interrupted by coughing and choking, he began to complain that I had neglected him so long – then he began to banter and tried to accuse me in a most innocent manner of mystical tendencies, which, since, it gave him pleasure, I allowed – then I conversed with his sister – then there were intervals of coughing – then came the moment to leave him in peace so I began to say goodbye, and he, gripping my hand, and shaking his hair from his brow, said: '. . . *I'm moving out!* . . . ' – and began to cough, which having heard, and knowing that it was good for his nerves sometimes to contradict him strongly, I employed just such an artificial tone and kissing him on the arm said, as one does to a person who is strong and manly: '... *You keep moving out every year ... and yet, God be praised, we still see you alive.*'

To which Chopin, concluding the words interrupted by the cough, said: '*I'm saying that I am moving out of this apartment to the Place Vendôme ...*'

This was my last conversation with him, for shortly afterwards he moved to the Place Vendôme and there died, but I did not see him again after that visit in the rue Chaillot ...

from
Vade-mecum
(1865)

Generalities

1

When like a butterfly the Artist-mind
In Spring of life inhales its air,
It can but say:
'The earth – is round – it is a sphere.'

2

But when autumnal shivers
Shake the trees and kill the flowers,
It must elaborate:
'Though somewhat – flattened – at the poles . . .'

3

Amid the varied charms
Of Eloquence and Rhyme
One – endures above the rest:

*   *   *   *   *   *   *   *

Granting objects proper names!

The Past

1

Death, pain, the *past*, are not God's,
But his who breaks the laws;
So – he can't bear the days;
And sensing evil, wants *remembrance* spurned!

2

But wasn't he like a child hurtling in a dray,
Crying: 'Oh! look, the oak's
Racing! . . . into the wood! . . . ',
– But the oak is still, the children borne away!

3

The *past* – is *now*, though somewhat far:
Behind the dray a farm,
Not *something somewhere*
Never known to man! . . .

In Verona

1

Above the house of Capulet and Montague,
Thunder-moved, washed in dew,
Heaven's gentle eye –

2

Looks on ruins of hostile city-states,
On broken garden gates,
And casts a star from on high –

3

It is for Juliet, cypresses whisper,
For Romeo that tear
Seeps through the tomb;

4

But men say knowingly and mock
That was no tear but a rock
Awaited by none!

Obscurity

1

He complains my speech is dark –
Has he ever lit the taper?
That remained his servant's task
(The many reasons hid from us).

2

The spark ignites the wick,
The melting wax engulfs the flame,
Its star-light slowly drowns,
Its sheen now bluish, on the wane.

3

You quickly think the light is lost
In the consummating flow –
Grant it faith, not just sparks and ash:
With your faith ... see how it glows!

4

You, who grudge a wretched moment –
Know the nature of my songs:
Their sacrificial flame will blaze
When the epoch's chill is gone!

Mercy

When tears flow, they wipe them with a cloth,
When blood flows, they run up with a sponge,
But when the spirit oozes under stress,
They will not rush with honest hands
Till God dries it with a thunder flash:
– Only then! . . .

The Sphinx

The Sphinx barred my way in a dark cave
Ever hungry for truths
Like a taxman, beggar or knave
Molesting travellers with cries of 'Truth!'

       *

'Man? . . . he's an ignorant callow
Priest . . . '
I replied

       *

And marvelling saw
The Sphinx pressed against the rock:
I slipped past alive!

Narcissus

I

Narcissus, mirroring a boastful face,
Cried, 'Let everyone note!
As I am supreme, so is Greece.'
Thereupon *Echo* spoke:

2

'These nymph-haunts, this lake,
And the depths of sapphire streams
Are not solely from your Greece,
But – from light, clouds and mists . . .

3

'Your shape, ponder, how? shimmering
Though you gaze in a crystal pool:
– Reflection comes from the distant *sun!*
Only the deep is – your constant *home*.'

Meanwhile

1

Generations pass,
Have space to move;
If fields are fenced,
A path is free.

2

Epochs pass,
They measure time,
But my days – delays
My years – to wait . . .

3

Haven't I now seen
The entire round?
Isn't all that's real
But a play's interval?

4

Life – the moment of death?
Youth – a day's hair turned white? . . .
My country – just
Her tragic fate?

Why Not in Chorus?

1

Round *God's* manger
The chosen sing;
But others at the door
Silently catch their breath . . .

2

And what of those
Just entering the town
Where the ear still rings
With *innocents' cries!* . . .

3

Sing you! who are chosen
There where He was born;
My ear is pierced
By the pursuing horn . . .

4

Sing in triumphant chorus
Your praises unto God – –
I? – could spoil your song:
    I have seen *blood!* . . .

Mysticism

I

A mystic? he's lost – of course!
Is there no *mystic* way?
It's a melancholy void,
A dream – till break of day! . . .

2

Does a highlander?
Lost on a clouded peak
Doubt the Alp is there

*   *   *   *   *   *

When lost – again?

Fate

Misfortune, like a wild beast, accosted man
And pierced him with its fateful eyes . . .
– Waits – –
Will man swerve?

II

But he gazed back like an artist
Who sizes up his model's form;
Noticing that he looks – *how?* to profit
From his foe:
It staggered with all its weight
– – And is gone!

Riddle

Are steel, rope or gold?
The shackles deepest soaked in
Tears and blood? –
The unseen! . . .

As when . . .

As when, silently, to surprise,
Someone throws violets in her eyes . . .

*

As when he gently rocks an acacia tree,
And scent of white
Petals like dawning light
Falls on white piano keys . . .

*

As when she stands at the porch
And into her hair the distant moon weaves
Itself, circling her brow with a shining wreath,
Or garlands it with silver sheaves . . .

*

As when idle talk with her
Is like a swallow's flight
That has its course yet strays everywhere,
A threat of summer thunder
Before lightning proclaims the tremor –
So . . .

. . . but I'll say nothing – in sorrow.

The Small Circle

How few people there are and hardly any
Willing to reveal themselves! ... – They pass – they
    pass –
They push each other away while dancing,
Or in intimate play, smoothly they cheat, deeply deceived;
Not *contemporaries*, not close, not even acquainted,
Grasping hands, slobbering in tight embrace.
The depth between them boils, grows oceanic
And on its froth – they; close how? ... only in name!
While the world says: '*They – are intimates – a family
    circle,*
Our – very own!' – the blue Heaven binds more truly
A thousand tribes in centuries of common slaughter,
Where at least one in each honestly believes in
A common Heaven. – Meanwhile they dance: bosom
    against bosom,
Polar-like unconscious of each other and apart;
It's enough one lamp shines over them all
And one fashion makes them all alike.
– '*Our very own!*' – what if someone were tracing
From on high a *life-map* like a *map of the globe*?
Mountains and deserts would move in a twinkling of
    an eye,
And the ocean disappear where one tiny tear-drop flows!

Feelings

Feelings – are like a cry full of war,
And like the current of whispering springs,
And like a funeral march . . .

                    *

And like a long plait of blond hair
On which a widower wears
A silver watch – – –

Gods and Man

I

Today authors are like God:
They breathe and a masterpiece is born;
The heavy plough soars in wingèd flight,
Toil is mere play!

2

The sun casts laurel-shade –
The friendly breeze complies,
Offering twenty years of fame –
For one auspicious day!

3

From Vergil's crafted lays
Men's inspiration rises still . . .
He! gave twenty years of toil
For one creative day!

Fervour

They say – beautiful were those times
When in a golden pillar rose the *sacred flame*,
And Rome looked to white virgins for protection:
Like the Senate, they ruled with the Caesars.
Meanwhile, the Druids and dark Lithuanian hordes
Sin-laden cursed the goat – their brows
Gilded by a living *Torch*, yet the sacred flame
Ended like all gifts which from Heavens came:
History followed legendary ages
And holy-fire ceased to guide the sages.
(We – by contrast – have a cheap phosphor match:
Grip it properly – depress its tip
And rub against your toe – a flame will leap.
The Turk takes the coiled hookah to his lip.)

The Mature Laurel

1

Only through solitary wars
Are future readers won;
You will neither dwell in halls
Nor command a private portal

2

In the Temple of your choice:
Others will unlock the grille –
And what? in life were *wings*,
History may bring to *heel!* ...

3

Today's screaming boasts,
Which you take for trumpet blasts? –
Are votes being cast ...
And silence is the *ballot-count*.

To a Deceased . . .

(On a tombstone)

Leave open behind you the door of this hall – –
Let us ascend higher! . . .
There *None* is and is a *Person:*
– Divisible, yet whole! . . .

      *

There – a million eyelashes covered with one tear,
'*Where art Thou?*' countless hearts sob,
– There – two nail-pierced feet
Fleeing the globe . . .

*   *   *   *   *   *   *   *   *   *   *

There – a million of my words; there – they fly too.

The Source

When I wandered in Hell which I do not sing
Since curses have first glued my lips,
Like ugly flies mad from the heat –
And also since each time I try – I yawn;
When wandering I passed a colonnade of boredom
Long and straight – also hallways of whims
And a cemetery of giants moving drowsily
Beneath cobbled stones and dying in the sands,
When my footsteps measured ante-chambers
Of silly-nerves which constantly try on clothes
And at wedding-time are never ready! . . .
– When I crossed thresholds of misery and portals of
    deceit
And was now passing insolent labyrinths of crime
Plastered everywhere with sentences of the Law,
I found myself at a spot where beneath my foot the lava
Cooled – so now I walked through air
And season and light that were truly God-less! . . .
– Like wheatfields charred by volcanoes
Or seas arrested and stinking,
Sea waves standing, gazing at each other, Sphinx-like,
Amazed at the strange habit of the deep,
– While above, some penguins
With open throats, thirst-parched,
And a couple of red stars which waning
Rush into the void . . .

      . . . there I went (unbelievably without rest! . . .)
I went there – where? . . . doubting . . . when a tiny plant
Pale and as if one clumsily embroidered,
Whispered to me: '. . . There is a spring . . . ' – and
    further in a ravine
I felt something like dampness.

From that side too
A bitter laugh and a stifled rustle came:
I perceived a Man with hands on his head –
As when one shifts all strength
Into one's feet – he was stamping on the Spring's blue
vein
Which like a ribbon had entwined his sandal
Or lay soiled in the dust where his foot had squashed it.
The human's laugh was wild – his accent strange:
Resembling the drum-beat following a coffin,
Echoing with sarcasm, hoarse with hate:
'See! . . . How the Creation-Spirit cleans my shoes! . . . '

Nerves

Yesterday I went to a place
Where people die of hunger –
Inspecting tomb-like rooms,
I slipped on an uncalculated stair!

*

It must have been a miracle – surely it was
That I clutched at a rotten plank . . .
(In it a nail as in the arms of a *cross!* . . .)
– I escaped with my life!

*

But carried – only half my heart:
Of mirth? . . . barely a trace!
I bypassed the crowd like a cattle mart;
I was sick of the world . . .

*

Today I must call on the Baroness
Who, sitting on a satin couch,
Entertains with largesse – –
But tell her what? . . .

. . . Mirrors will crack,
Candelabra shudder at the *realism*
And painted parrots
From beak to beak cry '*Socialism!*'
Along the length of the ceiling.

*

So: I will take a seat
Hat in hand – – then put it down,
And when the party's done,
Go home – a silent Pharisee.

The Last Despotism

'What news?' – 'Despotism's abolished! ... I have it all:
And here's the *despatch* ... '

                     'I trust you are well –
Be seated – *despatch* ... *it says?* ... Do take a chair!
But wait – I hear a mackintosh swishing in the hall –
Someone's coming! – It's the Baron – recovered from
    his fall ...
Please sit! – What news can the Baron share ... '

       *

'And that *despatch* ... it says what ...? A sugared drink?
Or perhaps an orange? ... ' 'In Greece –
Locusts – on Cyprus a village slipped over the brink –
Adelina Patti's singing in '*The Golden Fleece*' –
I see the orange's from Malta – it's very sweet.'
'Have another ... '

       *

           '... and how is Despotism in defeat??'

       *

But they've just announced the ex-chamberlain's wife
And her adopted son – 'What's your view of *nepotism?*
The boy's older than his mother by a year and a
    head ...
Here they are ...
       ... and now, this Despotism – is it dead? ... '

Finis

... Having dug out treachery beneath me
I end something of life in ending *mecum-vade,*
Made up of a *hundred* pearls threaded
Logically, shed tear into tear.
I stop the pen before ... before ...
The impatient reader stops:
Quietly I shut my notebook, like a cell-door – –

              *

Similarly, a *botanist* having his *herbarium* full
(When from the lowly moss the tiniest petal
Whispers about the deaths of creatures) and wanting
To sign the frontispiece ... writes ... *mortal!*

Late Poems
(1868–1881)

[Tell her – what?]

1

Tell her – what? . . . ah! win her admiration
With not much to say;
Something – of general truths: as that one day
And night mean – earth's full rotation!

2

That . . . during a single pulse-rate
The earth orbits through millions of miles –
The axis poles eternally grate:
Time – haunts the void – –

3

That a year . . . means – whole nature's tremor,
That seasons . . . not simply
How waters melt and freeze
And – that – – a heart beats? . . . for only an *hour!*

4

Tell – her that . . .
         . . . then discuss the weather –
Where is it warmer? colder where?
And add – what? the Fashion is this year
And not a word more.

1868

To Madame M. Going to Buy a Plate

1

There are generations, cities and tribes
   Melancholy and old –
Which have bequeathed not marvels untold
   But – a handful of pots!

2

In a Museum just such a pot
   Attracts a Lady with a parasol;
In Sicily she treads (and she is a Pole! . . .)
   Upon she knows not what! . . .

3

While Tribes one can't even mourn
   In their anonymous state
Vanish – like a butler after handing
   Her Ladyship a plate.

The 3rd day of 1869 (with a plate)

Lapidaria

SCULPTOR

Sculpture's
Whole secret:
A spirit – like lightning
In gesture caught – –

Marvels and wonders
And lifts its tiny palms
From this world's cradle
Towards the still uncaptured
In infinite space!

Only she who nurses
And he who's held a chisel;
Only she who dances
And he who's held an arm:
They only – and the earth's
Bosom sensing rain
Move the spirit's veil
– – Into a thrilling swirl!

MAECENAS

Since, master sculptor,
You so comprehend art's curious *mystery*,
Let my late wife Valerie
Have a monument from your hand – –
Let there be a stony angel
In a praying pose

Gazing at the base
Towards two crests
Crowned with a rose,

So that from every feeling breast
Should come a heartfelt sigh
Which (in a formula) means:
'*God forgive their sins!*'

1876

Undressed

(A Ballad)

1

You will not see her morning or night,
  She's *undressed* . . .

— — — — — — — — — — —

She must be sleeping! – let her acolytes
  Honestly stress,
Or she's up, but undressed,
  And in her bath.

2

Meanwhile three seamstresses with their needles
  And many a cobbler
Ignorantly tease the riddle
  Of her size.

3

Meanwhile somewhere at dawn
  Children march to school;
The ploughman tills, the Vistula flows,
  As do the Varta and the San.

4

Tender morning air, a balmy sight
  When the sky revives,
But alas! she's undressed
  Unable to lean out!

5

The world responds: 'Let her show
  Herself in a three-fold
Eastern-Western-motley dress
  Or a funeral gown!'

6

When I hear this, I have a different view
  Of the undressed:
How radiant is Diana's
  Uncovered breast!

7

Caught in brightness, Actaeon grows pale;
  Hounds ignore the blazing horns;
The Hyperborean Wood stands terror-struck,
  Quivering like a tottering shack . . .

8

While she of course both dignified and fair,
  Unarmed, undressed,
Is ever mindful that for all time
  Gods punish crime!

1881

To Bronisław Z.[5]

At the door of a dismal hut two tiny children
Played with splinters of a shattered pane;
A pane, whose fracture proved epoch-making in a village,
Where glaziers are scarce, but hailstones memorable,
As they leave branches broken, fields laid waste . . .
A wise man watched them delighting in rainbows
Cast by the glass; and thus a lens was born, while the
    mind's telescope
Focused on a milliard suns and tracks of worlds through
    the Milky Way!
– So, from the deeply provincial beauty of St Casimir's
    walls
I ask you – not *'are you familiar wth Venetian carnivals?'*
But are you – fellow-countryman! – amid all the curiosities
  · of festive Paris
Cognisant of the Feast-day of the Convent's Prioress?!

Old Michelet, whose youthful black eyes set against a
    snow-white mane
Are fresh in memory, had told me that, while many a
    worthy master
Had grasped the sacred and the beautiful, 'art's future lies
    in expressing goodness' . . .
– On the occasion when (I vividly recall) we discussed art,
The author of 'Wallenrod' (the master *miserly with theories,*
Preferring the creativity of immortal genius)
Said: 'Today, a master-craftsman sees not, lacks the
    insight,
To note the bearing and expression of a convent-sister
When, having received the Sacrament, she leaves the altar
    steps –
That's where the sources are! . . .' – That, I recall, is how
    the author of 'Dziady' spoke to me.

'What am I writing?' you ask; well, I'm writing you this
      letter –
But don't say I've sent you a token gift – *it's only poetry!*
Poetry without gold is poor – but gold without her,
I tell you, verily is *vanity of vanities* . . .
Varieties of opulence will crawl away and vanish,
Treasures and powers blow away, whole communities
      shake,
Of the things of this world only two will remain,
Two only: *poetry and goodness* . . . and nothing else . . .
Without them every skill will prove paper-thin,
So weighty is the duality of these two! . . .

You might think I'm writing this from Paris,
That city watered by the Seine,
Which by flickering gas-lamps every night
In its waves enfolds into cool shrouds a suicide or
      crime . . .

Look – here and there you see unremarkable walls.
Enter – it's late afternoon, you might think perhaps
You've strayed into remnants of a knights' monastery
Somewhere on Malta . . . and here or there through
      doors ajar
You'll have revealed a rusty sword hung from a wall,
Or a fierce and melancholy profile:
Like the shadow of a broken banner at a national funeral,
A near-centenarian in a confederate's cap
Has passed and faded into a corridor as long as
      nothingness –
You sense the ages ticking by like an ancient tower-clock,
Uncurious about the town for which from the clouds it
      strikes the hours.
Which century? Which misery? Which year?
Old Tacitus could hold a discourse with these men,
Learning how to draw morality from catastrophes.

Look! – here and there lovers of Him,
Who died on Golgotha, widowed for near
Two thousand years, now perambulate,
Doing good in His memory, their white wimples swaying
In step with their adoration duty-led.

Today, as it's the feast-day of the convent's leading lady,
Dozens of maidens blossom into as many smiles.
You notice extraordinary bustle – even the cock and hens
Disport themselves in the sun that scarcely warms the
    wall;
Let off its heavy chain, the dog has a sprightly gait.
There's something in the air. – Nearby is the great city
    of Paris,
Its two million mortals chasing after riches.
Here – *a dialogue* – you'd say, from the times of *Tirso*
    de Molina.
It's almost evening: a dressed-up girl with a moustache,
Clearly not drawn by a male hand – another
Like a bearded Jew, his awkwardness belied by her nimble
    trot.
Unabashed angels enact dramatic plots,
Like cherubs acting on familiar ground – and you can tell
They feel at ease with their paper wings, which then are
    stored
In cupboards till next year ... even though the girls
    mature,
And, I dare say, a handsome shape outgrows the wings.
Cracovian boys with maidens no bigger
Than twice this sheet – proceed to a lively dance,
Bowing, hat in hand, their gestures Polish,
Their homeland foreign ... (that, I recall, is how I'd play
With mother's blessing, as she lay in mortal pain! ...)

But now *the end* draws near; *the moral* and the baskets
Swiftly cleared, as oranges, nimbly caught

By hands failing to grip the fruits' full rotundity,
Enlarge their rarity, size and worth.

– Happiness, you see, my dear! – exists – so does Poland –
    and Humanity
(Take the oranges as proof . . . hasn't Newton's apple
Taught us significant truths? . . .) – there's also art's
    essential strength,
Alive when able to idealize the here and now.
Let that also make you indulgent toward hexameters:
'*Exsul eram, requiesque mihi, non fama!* . . . '
    Vale – –

1879

Notes

1 (p. 28)   This purported quotation from *Hamlet* echoes rather Prospero's celebrated speech in *The Tempest* (Act IV, Scene i). The most that can be said is that in Norwid's poem, as in *Hamlet* (and of course in *The Tempest*) the theme of reality and appearance dominates.

2 (p. 31)   The poet Jan Kochanowski (1530–1584) of Czarnolas.

3 (p. 35)   General Józef Bem (1794–1850) was a leading figure in Poland's 1830 uprising against Russia and in the Hungarian uprising of 1848 against the Habsburg Empire; he then hoped to help the Turks against Russia, but died prematurely in Syria. After the failed Hungarian uprising against Soviet Russia in 1956, *Nowa Kultura*, Poland's leading Party literary weekly, printed Norwid's elegy in silent tribute.

4 (p. 39)   The Emir (1807–1883), though a Muslim, defended the Christian community against a pogrom in Syria in 1860.

5 (p. 91)   In 1877 Norwid reluctantly moved to St Casimir's, a Polish convent in the Ivry district on the outskirts of Paris, run by Mother Teofila Mikułowska of the Sisters of Mercy, whose feast-day, referred to in the poem, fell on 28th December. The establishment catered both for army veterans and orphans. At St Casimir's in 1879 Norwid wrote 'To Bronisław Z.', that is, addressed Bronisław Zaleski, one of his few remaining loyal friends. 'The author of *Wallenrod*' and 'the author of *Dziady* [The Ancestors]' is Adam Mickiewicz; Michelet is the French historian; the closing lines, 'I, an exile, seek rest, not fame', are from Ovid's *Tristia*, also written in exile. Norwid died at St Casimir's in 1883.